ADELYN BIRCH

30 COVERT EMOTIONAL MANIPULATION TACTICS

How Manipulators Take Control in Personal Relationships

Copyright © 2015 by Adelyn Birch

All rights reserved. No part of this publication may be reproduced, stored or transmitted in any form or by any means, electronic, mechanical, photocopying, recording, scanning, or otherwise without written permission from the publisher. It is illegal to copy this book, post it to a website, or distribute it by any other means without permission.

First edition

ISBN: 978-1-52-292284-1

This book was professionally typeset on Reedsy. Find out more at reedsy.com

Labyrinths twist and turn,
but they have a beginning and an end, through
darkness into light.

~ Ariana Franklin, The Serpent's Tale

Contents

About the Author ii
Reviews from Readers of 30 Covert Emotional Manipulation... iii
1 What is Covert Emotional Manipulation? 1
2 How Can You Tell if You're Being Manipulated? 19 Signs 4
3 30 Covert Emotional Manipulation Tactics 11
4 I Refuse to Have This Discussion! All About Invalidation 42
5 The Most Powerful Motivator on the Planet 49
6 Intimacy or Intensity? A Relationship Litmus Test 55
7 Your Basic Rights In Relationships 59
8 Now What? 62

About the Author

Adelyn Birch is the author of the unique and popular website, *Psychopaths and Love,* which she created for people who were victimized by psychopaths in personal relationships, as she was. Visitors find information, insight, understanding, support, and healing — and perhaps most importantly, learn that they are not alone.

You can visit the website at PsychopathsandLove.com.

Other books by the author:

Boundaries: Loving Again After a Pathological Relationship

Psychopaths and Love

MORE Psychopaths and Love

202 Ways to Spot a Psychopath in Personal Relationships

Reviews from Readers of 30 Covert Emotional Manipulation Tactics

"Clear, concise, accurate portrayal of complex subject matter impacting many people. I appreciate the accessibility to the general public of a topic that is often overlooked, but impacts morale not only in romantic relationships, but in the family, at work and in myriad social situations."

"Impressive! Short, direct, and thought-provoking. I only wish I had read it years ago! Every young person should read this before dating!"

"Shockingly on point! Easy read, really opened my eyes. Helps you take steps in the right direction."

"This short read was very concise and to the point - exactly what most people need to hear right away when in the middle of a debilitating manipulative relationship. Having several other books on the topic, this was a wonderful departure. This small manual is filled with more information, frankly, then page 200+ of the current book that I'm reading on the same subject. Kudos to the author for putting together a truly valuable reference manual that really cuts to the chase, and helps to dissolve some of the feelings you may not be able to put into words otherwise!"

"Great book! Incredibly informative! It helped me realize what was happening in my relationship. It gave me the strength to move on and leave. I am so grateful I found this book."

"Gain your power back learning to recognize when someone is trying to take it away. I am a survivor of a very skilled covert emotional manipulator. Trying to regain mental health and undue the damage caused by such veiled abuse has been the most challenging thing I have faced in my life. This book is clearly written and the contents in this book are very powerful in that it helps arm you against becoming entangled with such dangerous people in the future."

"Very educational! This book really made me open my eyes and see what has been happening to me during my entire marriage. I felt like she was writing about my life!"

"Thankful for the willingness of authors like Adelyn Birch who put into words the craziness that I survived and thankfully escaped. Highly recommend this book."

"I am alive again! I was experiencing hell only just yesterday. I was being tortured on a daily basis for almost 4 years. As I began reading it, I immediately felt relief and peace as I understood I was a victim of ALL the tactics explained in this book. You can be killed and still be alive. I have been enlightened and will move forward. Today I woke up happy, energetic and grateful to have a second chance at life!"

"This author nails it. Some examples were direct quotes from people I know, so I know I am not alone in having been manipulated. It is directly applicable to my life and gives excellent guidance for how to recognize and therefore avoid manipulations in the future. I am recommending it to a number of my friends."

"I did not realize how detrimental this type of abuse was until I experienced it myself. This book brought to light the true culprit of the issues and manipulation I went through in my past relationship. It has freed me from the emotional entanglement since reading and I finally feel like me again.

Thank you!"

"This short and direct work is worth your time. In many lives people get worked over without ever knowing it. Some of us are used by 'friends' over and over yet we don't see it. This book points out a lot of things we should be very aware of in order for successful relationships. Well done."

"BRAVO! Everyone should read this.. if you're in a controlling relationship, man or woman, this will help you spell it out. "

"Eye opening for sure! This was like reading a textbook of my doubts, fears, and insecurities. I can finally be free from the bondage."

"Five Stars. Where was this book before!"

"A must read for anyone in a toxic relationship. I really enjoyed this book. It opened a door for me that will free me from all manipulators. I highly recommend it."

"I have read multiple books on abusive relationships and NPD in order to discover what I'm actually dealing with, knowing it's not been normal. This book covered everything so succinctly and could've saved me so much time had I found it earlier."

"Shocking. As I read this book I was shocked to see all these confusing emotions I have, all the self doubt and questioning my sanity are a result of my being manipulated."

"Very insightful. I liked how the author cut right to the meat. If I had my way this book would be required high school or college reading."

"If you suspect you miht be dealing with a manipulator, MUST READ!"

1

What is Covert Emotional Manipulation?

Until you realize how easy it is for your mind to be manipulated, you remain the puppet of someone else's game.

~ Evita Ochel

Covert emotional manipulation tactics are underhanded methods of control. These deceptive tactics act to change your behavior and perceptions. Covert manipulation operates under the level of your conscious awareness. Victims usually do not realize they are being manipulated while it is happening. That is exactly why it is important to become aware of the methods manipulators use.

Who are these manipulative people?

The most skillful and dangerous manipulators are those included in psychology's "dark triad." Psychopathic, narcissistic, and Machiavellian personalities lack empathy and manipulate in a planned and purposeful way for their own personal gain, no matter the cost to someone else. They are callous, insensitive, aggressive, and opportunistic individuals who use others and act out against them to achieve their own ends. It is entirely possible to have a member of the dark triad as your partner, friend, neighbor, relative, coworker or boss. They attempt to hide who they really are by creating a seemingly normal—and often a charming and likeable—persona, but their malicious intent remains active behind the mask. These individuals are detrimental to the mental health of anyone who has close contact with them.

People without serious psychological disorders also use manipulation to get what they want, often without malicious intent and sometimes without any awareness of what they are doing. It is said that we are all guilty of using manipulation on occasion instead of communicating our needs and desires in a direct way. There is a significant difference between someone who is a pathological manipulator and someone who uses manipulation to get what they want from time to time. Pathological manipulators have no other way to relate to others and nothing real to offer in a relationship, such as love and intimacy. There is no way to change them.

Manipulation undermines your ability to consciously make decisions and take actions in your own best interest, in accordance with your personal values and boundaries. In other words, manipulation gets you to do things you wouldn't otherwise do.

At its worse, emotional manipulation methodically wears down your self-worth and self-confidence and damages your trust in your own perceptions. It can make you unwittingly compromise yourself to the point of losing your self-respect and developing a warped concept of reality. With your defenses weakened or completely disarmed in this manner, you are left even more vulnerable to further manipulation.

A skilled emotional manipulator gets you to put your sense of self-worth and emotional well-being into his or her hands. Once you're tricked into making that grave mistake, they methodically chip away at your identity and wreak havoc on your psychological health, and serious harm results.

WHAT IS COVERT EMOTIONAL MANIPULATION?

In order to be successful, a malicious manipulator must know your vulnerabilities, conceal their aggressive intentions and behavior, and be ruthless enough not to care what harm their manipulation causes you. Taking control and getting what they want are all that matters.

Becoming aware of the tactics manipulators use enables you to identify concealed aggression. But it is not always easy to do, because manipulators count on your trust, doubt and strong emotions –guilt, fear, love and shame – to prevent you from thinking clearly and seeing the manipulation. In many cases they manufacture these emotions purposely for that reason. That's how manipulators get away with what they do. Therefore, it is very important for you to recognize when you are doubting your own perceptions or intuition, or experiencing an emotion that makes you vulnerable to manipulation.

Although this book focuses on romantic relationships, the manipulation tactics described are simply that, manipulation tactics. Many are the same methods employed by manipulative friends, family members, coworkers, bosses, neighbors, and even children.

2

How Can You Tell if You're Being Manipulated? 19 Signs

Emotional manipulation can be so subtle and undercover that it can control you for a long time before you figure out what's happening, if you ever do at all. Some manipulators are highly skilled. They are described as puppet masters, and you could unknowingly become a puppet if you don't know the signs.

As your strings are pulled this way and that, you do just what the puppet master wants you to do. You think you're acting from your own free will, but you are not.

If you are a victim of manipulation you probably know something is wrong, but you're not quite sure what it is. You might even suspect you are being manipulated but you do not know for sure if you are, or how it's being done. One thing you do know is that you want answers. Are you being manipulated or not? How can you tell?

Actually, it is easier and more obvious than you might think.

It's smart to learn the techniques of covert emotional manipulation, and you will do just that in the next chapter. But the truth is you don't have to know anything at all about the techniques to know if you're being manipulated. *You only need to look at yourself to know if manipulation is at play.*

Manipulation is detrimental and has profound negative effects on us, even if we don't know it's happening. Those negative effects are the evidence left when the crime of manipulation has taken place.

If you are in a relationship and notice any of the following signs, there is a high probability you are being manipulated:

- Your joy at finding love has turned into the fear of losing it. Your feelings have gone from happiness and euphoria to anxiety, sadness, and even desperation.

- Your mood depends entirely on the state of the relationship, and you are experiencing extreme highs and lows.

- You are unhappy in the relationship and uncertain about it much of the time, yet you dread losing it because you experience blissful happiness every now and then.

- You feel like you are responsible for ruining the best thing that ever happened to you, yet you are not sure how.

- Your relationship feels very complex, although you do not know why. When talking to others about it, you might find yourself saying "It's hard to explain. It's just really complicated."

- You continually obsess about the relationship, analyzing every detail repeatedly in a desperate attempt to "figure it out." You talk about it all the time to anyone who will listen. It doesn't do any good.

- You never feel sure of where you stand with your partner, which leaves you in a perpetual state of uncertainty and anxiety.

- You frequently ask your partner if something is wrong. It really does feel as if something is wrong, but you are not sure what it is.

- You are frequently on the defensive. You feel misunderstood and have the need to explain and defend yourself.

- You seem to have developed a problem with trust, jealousy, insecurity, anger, or over-reacting, which your partner has pointed out to you on many occasions.

HOW CAN YOU TELL IF YOU'RE BEING MANIPULATED? 19 SIGNS

- You feel ongoing anger at, or resentment for, your partner.

- You have become a detective. You scour the web for information about your partner, keep a close eye on his or her social media accounts, and feel a need to check their web search history, texts, or emails. When they are not at home, you have a desire to verify their whereabouts as you worry about where they *really* are.

- You feel that you do not truly know how to make your partner happy. You try hard but nothing seems to work, at least not for long. You used to make them very happy and you're not sure what's changed.

- Expressing negative thoughts and emotions feels restricted or even forbidden, so you try to keep them to yourself. You feel frustrated at being unable to talk about things that are bothering you.

- You don't feel as good about yourself as you did before the relationship. You feel less confident, less secure, less intelligent, less sane, less trusting, less attractive, or in some other way "less than" what you were before.

- You always feel you are falling short of your partner's expectations. You feel inadequate.

- You often feel guilty and you find yourself apologizing a lot. You continually try to repair damage you believe you've caused. You blame yourself for your partner pulling away from you. You cannot understand why you keep sabotaging the relationship.

- You carefully control your words, actions, and emotions around your partner to keep him or her from withdrawing their affection again.

- At times, you erupt like an emotional volcano filled with anger and frustration or even rage and hostility. You have never acted this way before and vow that you will stop, but no matter how hard you try, it keeps happening.

- You do things you aren't really comfortable with or that go against your values, limits or boundaries, in order to make your partner happy and keep the relationship intact.

You should have your answer.

There is one caveat. If your past relationships have had an ongoing pattern of insecurity, mistrust, and fear of abandonment, you may have an issue that would benefit from professional intervention, such as an insecure attachment style or a past trauma that leads you into serial relationships with members of the dark triad.

You might be wondering how you or anyone else could stay in a relationship that causes fear, anxiety, depression, self-doubt, confusion, and frustration. Wouldn't you know something is terribly wrong? Why would you stay?

First, relationships don't start out this way. In fact, the relationship probably got off to an exceptional start. He or she seemed like your perfect partner—maybe even your soul mate—and the honeymoon phase was idyllic. When things took a turn for the worse, you had no idea what was really going on. Naturally, you would try to work things out and regain what once was so promising and wonderful. Having been manipulated into blaming yourself for the problems, you hang on and desperately try to repair the damage you believe you caused, to regain your partner's love. Your loyalty seems to pay off and you and your partner are once again close and loving... for a while. It becomes a cycle, one you may not be aware of.

Second, manipulation begins slowly and insidiously, and gradually escalates.

"Manipulation is an evolving process over time," according to Harriet B. Braiker, PhD., author of *Who's Pulling Your Strings*. Braiker says victims are controlled through a series of promised gains and threatened losses, covertly executed through a variety of manipulation tactics. In other words, the manipulation builds gradually as the abuser creates uncertainty and doubt by going back and forth from giving you what you desire and threatening to take it away.

This cycle will be discussed in more detail in the chapter on the manipulation tactic of intermittent reinforcement.

Joe Navarro, M.A., a 25-year veteran of the FBI and author of the book *Dangerous Personalities*, writes "In the end, it doesn't matter how you got into that relationship, it is the realization that it is one-sided, exploitative, and toxic that counts. The questions that need to be asked are very simple. 'Are they using their charms or behavior to control you or others for their own benefit? Are they manipulating you? Are they doing things that hurt you or put you at risk? Do you feel like this relationship is one sided? Are you hurting in this relationship?' If the answer to these questions is yes, it is time to untangle yourself from the toxic strings that control you so you can get your life back. Take heed - you have no social obligation to be victimized – ever."

Emotional manipulation is emotional abuse. A person who controls your feelings and behavior with manipulation does not value or respect you or care about your well-being. Leave the relationship if at all possible, and seek professional counseling if necessary. Involvement with a skilled manipulator can result in serious and lasting harm.

Only you can decide if a relationship is worthwhile and salvageable or if it is detrimental to you and needs to end.

The last chapter will provide you with resources that will enable you to learn how to deal with manipulators.

Awareness is one of your primary defenses against covert manipulation. With that thought, what follows are descriptions of thirty covert emotional manipulation tactics. A few of them will be explored in more depth in chapters that follow.

You have no social obligation to be victimized — ever.

~Joe Navarro, veteran FBI agent

3

30 Covert Emotional Manipulation Tactics

1. Intermittent Reinforcement

The more infrequently the crumbs of love are offered, the more hooked you are. You become conditioned, like a rat in a cage.

~ Unknown

Intermittent reinforcement is an extremely powerful and effective manipulation tactic. In fact, psychology experts consider it the most powerful motivator in existence. Using this tactic, the manipulator "motivates" the victim to behave, think or feel the way he or she wants them to.

Intermittent reinforcement occurs when a manipulator gives his victim positive reinforcement—attention, praise, appreciation, affection, sex, adoration, declarations of love—only on a random basis. They may give positive reinforcement in response to a behavior they are trying to increase, or they can withhold it to create uncertainty, anxiety and longing in the victim.

Intermittent reinforcement creates a climate of doubt, fear and anxiety that compels the victim to persistently seek acts of positive reinforcement from the manipulator that will alleviate their angst. When the reward of positive reinforcement is given, it is very powerful. It floods the brain with dopamine and other feel-good neurotransmitters and hormones. It creates addiction.

If you're a victim of this tactic, you will sense the manipulator is withdrawing. He or she is not giving you the attention and affection that they used to, and you will fear that something is wrong and that you are losing them. If you ask them if something is wrong, they will deny it or blame you. At some point the manipulator will act once again like the attentive, romantic, interested and loving person they once were. Your anxiety and doubt are relieved, and you are on top of the world. But then they withdraw again, and you are consumed with anxiety once more. By using intermittent reinforcement the manipulator will have you riding an emotional roller coaster, your moods and emotional well-being dependent upon whether he or she is withholding from you or rewarding you.

The manipulator does this on purpose to increase his or her power and control over you and to make you ever more desperate for their love, attention or approval. You will have become the proverbial lab rat living for a randomly dispensed morsel. The rat thinks of nothing else, and either will you.

Your bond with the manipulator will become stronger in response to intermittent reinforcement, along with your desire to please them and your fear of losing them.

This is malicious manipulation at its worse.

Intermittent reinforcement is explored in more depth in chapter five.

2. Negative Reinforcement

Using the tactic of negative reinforcement, the manipulator stops doing something you don't like when you start doing something he or she does like. This makes it more likely that you will do what they like in the future.

For example, you behave in some way the manipulator does not like. Perhaps you go out with your friends on Friday nights or refuse to participate in some sexual activity you are averse to. In response, they engage in behavior that hurts you, such as withholding affection or giving you the silent treatment. The manipulator stops withholding affection or giving you the silent treatment when you start acting the way he wants, such as promising to give up your Friday get-togethers or engaging in the sexual activity he desires.

It's very simple. The manipulator knows you are likely to give in eventually in order to stop his or her hurtful actions. It is an effective way to get you to behave the way they want you to, and to make you more likely to behave that way again.

3. Backing Into an Emotional Corner

You always overreact! You're unstable! You have a problem with anger! You're crazy!

A manipulator will say such things after intentionally causing you to have an emotional meltdown. The purpose is to create a confusing and emotional scene that will distract you from an issue you confronted the manipulator about. The issue instead becomes your apparent emotional instability. This tactic also allows the manipulator to gain more power and control.

Here's an example of how this tactic is put into play:

You are upset by something the manipulator did and you confront him or her about it. Perhaps he did something that aroused your suspicion or angered you. The manipulator does not want to confront the issue at hand, so he obfuscates it by turning the focus onto you by using your emotions against you. He does not mention the issue you brought up; instead, he immediately shifts the focus to your apparent insecurity or jealousy or suspicious nature, which he says is unacceptable.

You become defensive, frustrated and upset. The manipulator seizes on your emotional upset, and says something like "You already know I won't tolerate you raising your voice at me," or "Is it PMS time again?" or "You're not trying to pick another fight, are you?" or "I can see you're headed toward one of your meltdowns." This will increase your frustration and make you become even more emotional.

Then the manipulator will tell you that he can't deal with this anymore, that he's becoming tired of your drama and your overreaction. At this point (if you haven't done so already) you'll have an emotional meltdown and then collapse into frustrated sobs. Then the manipulator will announce that you're unstable or crazy or abusive or that you have an anger management problem, and says that he will leave you if you can't get your yourself under control.

The manipulator backed you into an emotional corner. Predictably, you came out swinging.

The manipulator will storm off in feigned anger and begin a protracted episode of the silent treatment, which is yet another way to avoid the real issue (and another manipulation tactic).

You are ashamed at how you acted and feel disappointed in yourself. You can't understand why you keep going off the deep end. You will come to believe that you actually do have an emotional problem, one that is sabotaging your previously wonderful relationship. You vow to yourself not to let it happen again, but suppressing your frustration only guarantees that your buttons will be even easier to push next time.

You unwittingly enter a vicious cycle with no way out.

When you've been backed into an emotional corner, acting out does not mean you're crazy or that you have an anger management problem. It means you're a normal person reacting to an intensely stressful situation. But when you have an emotional reaction to that stress, you're made to believe you have a problem.

Your emotional reactions to manipulation are not the problem—the manipulation is the problem.

This is psychological warfare at its lowest.

4. Shifting The Focus

Shifting the focus usually happens along with the tactic of backing into an emotional corner, but it can happen even if you confront a manipulator in a matter-of-fact way, without emotional drama, and he or she has something to hide.

With this tactic, you attempt to talk about a concern you have with the manipulator, such a suspicion that he or she is cheating on you. Instead of dealing with the stated concern, the manipulator simply denies your allegations, expresses incredulity that you could even think such a thing about them, and then discusses the real problem—your supposed character flaw, such as insecurity or jealousy—making it clear that they find it highly unattractive. Since this is yet another tactic that makes you believe the relationship is in trouble and it is your fault, you learn to not ask questions and instead doubt your suspicions and yourself.

An interesting and surprisingly common example of shifting the focus:

You have strong suspicions that your partner is having an affair. Gaining access to his or her email or text messages reveals evidence that supports your suspicions. You confront the manipulator with the evidence, and the focus is immediately shifted to your invasion of his or her privacy and (ironically to your lack of trust. Somehow, it works. Manipulators will try anything, no matter how outrageous it may be, and they are often successful.

When you are immersed in the confusing world they create, normal rules don't seem to apply anymore.

5. Premature Disclosure

Using this tactic, manipulators reveal deeply personal information about themselves early on in the relationship to create a false sense of intimacy, for the purpose of gaining your trust and creating the illusion of a bond.

The manipulator's self-disclosure can include their thoughts, feelings, goals, fears, dreams, embarrassments, likes and dislikes, painful memories, and successes and failures. You'll feel free to reveal personal things about yourself in return, which the manipulator is counting on.

The manipulator will also falsely claim to like the same things you do, feel the same way you do, or have had the very same thing happen, leading you to feel amazed at all you have in common. There is also the opportunity for the manipulator to impress the target by disclosing achievements, riches, and seemingly selfless acts of philanthropy, compassion, and kindness.

In normal relationships, self-revelation involves vulnerability because it carries a risk of rejection—but when it is met with acceptance and understanding, it creates genuine emotional intimacy and trust. Manipulators know this and use it to their advantage.

6. Triangulation

Never let the other person use absence, or create pain and conflict, to keep you, the seduced, on tenterhooks.

~ Robert Greene, The Art of Seduction

Triangulation is a devious and effective tactic in a manipulator's arsenal. The manipulator creates a triangle between you, him or her, and some third person outside of your relationship. It is intended to make you feel insecure about the relationship, and therefore more eager to please the manipulator in order to keep him or her around.

The manipulator will figuratively (or literally) bring another man or woman into the relationship in some way. They might talk casually—and frequently—about an old flame, a coworker, or someone they bump into regularly on their morning coffee run. Or they might obviously flirt with someone in front of you. Their interest in the other person creates insecurity. If they make subtle unfavorable comparisons between you and the outside person, which they're apt to do, that makes it much worse.

If you confront them they will deny interest in the other person and tell you that the real problem is your insecurity or low self-esteem. Where have you heard that before?

It is not uncommon for the manipulator to be grooming the other person as his or her next target, while conveniently using that person to devalue and manipulate you.

For example, the manipulator might flirt with another woman in front of you so he can build his relationship with her while causing you to behave jealously, which can then be used against you as the reason to end your relationship.

In a healthy relationship, you will know where you stand with your partner. A manipulator creates an ongoing sense of uncertainty, which leads to ongoing emotional angst.

7. Blaming The Victim

You've saddled me with a lie I never deserved... you led me to believe I was responsible.

~ The Prize, Irving Wallace

With this tactic, the manipulator holds the victim responsible for the problems in a relationship. This tactic is a powerful means of putting you on the defense (which makes you look guilty) or making you believe you truly are the one to blame.

As the relationship goes bad, and when it finally comes to an end, the manipulator will claim that you are the one at fault. They may even manipulate mutual friends and family into believing you are the one to blame, turning them against you. Just when you need support, you find yourself with little or none. Skilled manipulators always pretend they are the actual victim.

8. Indirect Insults

Always remember, he knows EXACTLY which buttons to push.

~ Unknown

Name-calling and insults are directly and obviously aggressive and abusive. An underhanded way to disguise aggression and abuse is to deliver it without the expected angry or sarcastic tone of voice and instead make it sound like teaching, helping, giving advice or offering solutions. It appears to be a sincere attempt to help you, but it's actually the opposite. It's a powerful way to undermine your confidence in yourself and your abilities.

For example, a manipulator might tell you that you would be less boring as a dance partner if you took a few lessons (when you never knew he considered you boring to dance with); or she might tell you that she thinks you're a perfectly "adequate" partner when you question her about what you sense as her emotional withdrawal; or he might say that he loves it when you wear that dress because it has such a slimming effect on you.

These indirect insults are sometimes called backhanded compliments, but that doesn't do justice to the effect this tactic has when the manipulator—someone who you trust and who you believe has your best interests at heart—zeros in on your biggest insecurities or disparages what you consider your best qualities.

9. Insinuating Comments or Compliments

The manipulator "innocently" makes what is actually a carefully crafted insinuating comment designed to evoke an uncomfortable emotional response. When you take offense, he will tell you that is not what he intended. The statement is usually disguised as a compliment, but it's one that does not feel very flattering. It is disguised enough, though, for you to believe you might have misunderstood.

The manipulator knows what will bother you, and he or she will enjoy dropping a bomb like this and watching the fallout. Their comment is designed to have several possible meanings, many of which will inspire hurt feelings and doubt. You may feel flummoxed and left without a meaningful response when you first hear it because it has so many possible interpretations.

As an example, your partner smiles and says, "You know what? You could make a lot of money as a prostitute!" after you've had sex with him. When you question him he will tell you he meant it as a compliment. But you will wonder what he really meant, for a long time to come. For the example given, you might wonder why your partner was thinking about prostitutes when he was in bed with you; why he knows so much about prostitution in the first place; what he really thinks of you; and the amount you should put on the bill you're tempted to send to him. And you will also wonder if he was just complimenting you on how great he thinks you are in bed, as he said he was.

Comments like these will go to work on you and provide the fuel for plenty of resentment, future arguments and relationship insecurity. It's easy for the manipulator to make it look like a misunderstanding on your part, but therein lies the clue: the manipulator says he or she meant it as an innocent compliment, one that you simply misunderstood. Of course you did; a compliment doesn't usually hurt your feelings or leave you feeling bewildered.

10. Guilt

Your conscience and your desire to be a good person can be used to control you. A skilled manipulator can make you feel incredibly guilty for not doing something they want you to do, by getting you to feel that you *should* do it even if you really don't want to do.

Many of us are conditioned to feel guilt by our family, religion, or culture, so it is easy for manipulators to make us feel it, too. Being able to feel guilt means we have a conscience. It's not a bad thing, except when it's exploited.

Guilt is a negative emotion experienced when we believe we have harmed someone or when something we've done, or failed to do, made someone think poorly of us. Our natural reaction is to apologize, make amends, and act in a way that will make the other person think highly of us again, which means acting in the way that person wants us to act.

Guilt is closely related to shame and anxiety. It is an uncomfortable emotion, so we are highly motivated to avoid it. We evade the torment of guilt by behaving the way others expect us to. Manipulators know this all too well and use it to their advantage.

The following are examples of statements that can send us on a guilt trip:

"I can't believe you would even think that I would lie to you!"

"How can you feel that way after all I've done for you?"

"Don't worry, I guess I'll manage somehow if you won't help me out."

"If you really loved me, you would _____" (fill in the blank with anything a manipulator wants you to do, that you do not want to do.)

11. Shame

We feel shame when someone communicates to us that we are not worthy of respect. A manipulator can make a victim feel shame by expressing disgust or disappointment, using sarcasm or put-downs, or by comparing us to someone else they claim to think is better in some way.

Shame is a very powerful tool for a manipulator. Few emotional states are more painful than shame. We feel guilty for what we *do*, but we feel shame for what we *are*. Shame is a feeling of deep humiliation, and some manipulators enjoy making their victim feel humiliated. It places them in a superior position.

According to clinical psychologist Gershen Kaufman, "Shame is the most disturbing experience individuals ever have about themselves; no other emotion feels more deeply disturbing because in the moment of shame the self feels wounded from within."

In relationships, we feel shame from anything we say or do that we believe weakens the bond or causes rejection. Many of the manipulation tactics described in this book accomplish one or both of those.

Shame can turn into the pervasive belief that you are in some way inherently defective or unacceptable, so this manipulation tactic can cause serious psychological harm. Your sense of self-worth will suffer, and that will have a negative effect on all aspects of your life.

12. Empty Words

The basic tool for the manipulation of reality is the manipulation of words.

~Philip K. Dick

Manipulators are liars who think nothing of making a promise or commitment they have no intention of keeping. They are also consummate seducers who can turn on the charm and tell you exactly what you want to hear:

"I love you."

"You're so special to me."

"I don't know how I got so lucky."

"I've waited my whole life for you."

When a manipulator utters these words they are backed up by nothing, but you may not notice that his or her actions are telling a very different story.

Using empty words to fulfill your need for approval, love, validation, admiration, appreciation or reassurance gives a manipulator incredible power over you. They tell you what you want to hear in order to get what they want.

Always remember: **Actions speak louder than words.**

If you feel confused because someone tells you that they love you but they don't act like they do, judge them by their actions alone. You will have your answer.

13. Crazymaking

It's called crazymaking for a reason. When using this tactic, a manipulator simply denies ever having said something they did indeed say. It could happen a month later, a year later or a minute later.

You know the manipulator said it, they know they said it, and they know you know they said it. But none of that matters; they will simply insist they never said whatever it was they said, and hope you believe them.

If you feel you need to have a tape recorder running whenever you speak with a particular person, you are a victim of crazymaking.

14. Gaslighting

Using the tactic of gaslighting, the manipulator denies, and therefore invalidates, reality. Invalidating reality distorts or undermines the victim's perceptions of their world and can even lead them to question their own sanity.

"I don't know where you got that idea."

"It's all in your head."

"You've always had a bad memory!"

"That never happened. Are you crazy?"

"You must be trying to confuse me."

"You're imagining things."

"I have no idea what you're talking about."

This kind of deception seems like it would be obvious, but it usually begins very gradually and increases in frequency and severity over time. It leads to anxiety, depression and confusion. Victims eventually question their 'version' of reality. When they no longer trust their own perceptions, they rely on the manipulator to define reality and can no longer function independently. Having rendered the victim completely helpless and lacking any self-confidence, the manipulator is able to exercise total domination and get whatever it is they want, whether it is a feeling of superiority, financial control or sexual benefits.

Examples of gaslighting:

A manipulator claims that the victim is mistaken in her belief that he wanted a committed, long-term relationship, even though everything he did and said created that belief.

A manipulator says something in an angry tone of voice, but when the victim becomes upset the manipulator denies having used an angry tone.

A manipulator deliberately upsets a victim, and then mocks them or puts them down for "overreacting."

A manipulator purposely withholds certain details, and later tries convincing the victim that they did indeed tell them the missing details.

A manipulator moves items from one place to another and then denies having done so.

A manipulator asserts something untrue with enough conviction and intensity that the victim believes it.

You might be a victim of gaslighting if you apologize often, have trouble making decisions, have changed significantly over the course of the relationship, feel you're in a constant state of bewilderment, or have become reclusive and withdrawn.

Gaslighting is even more effective when used in combination with other techniques of manipulation. You may have noticed that many other tactics include the element of denying a victim's reality.

15. Minimizing

The manipulator uses this tactic to convince you that something she did that was wrong really wasn't as bad as you think it is. She will tell you that you're making a big deal out of nothing or that you're exaggerating or overreacting when you confront her about her wrongdoing.

You can be sure that if a manipulator uses this tactic, they will engage in the same bad behavior in the future.

16. The Silent Treatment

Supposedly because of something you did, the manipulator refuses to communicate with you and uses emotional or physical withdrawal as punishment. This is commonly called the silent treatment, stonewalling, or withholding.

It conveys contempt and communicates that you are not worth the manipulator's acknowledgement of your existence, let alone his or her time, love, attention or consideration, according to Steve Becker, LCSW. He writes, "The silencer's aim is, above all, to silence communication. More specifically, it is to render the other invisible and, in so doing, induce feelings of powerlessness and shame."

Becker says the silent treatment "is a technique of torture. This may sound hyperbolic, but human beings need (on the most basic level) recognition of their existence. The withholding of this recognition, especially if protracted, can have soul-warping consequences on personality."

Giving the silent treatment is an effective way for a manipulator to get you to behave as he or she wants you to.

17. Lying

Lying is the granddaddy of manipulation tactics. Purposeful manipulators lie frequently and without remorse, and have an arsenal of lying styles to work from. Others may feel remorse but will lie anyway to get what they want.

Manipulators will say anything to get results. Many are expert liars who lie convincingly, frequently, and with impunity.

Basically, a lie is a false statement deliberately presented as the truth. But there are many other ways to lie that go far beyond simply making a blatantly false statement. Those statements often work, though, because we can't believe that someone we trust would look us in the eye and tell us such a brazen, bald-faced lie.

Lies of omission are one of the more subtle forms of lying. Instead of making a deceptive statement, the liar withholds the truth. For example, the manipulator may not tell you he's married if he thinks it would stop you from becoming involved with him. He didn't tell you he wasn't married; he just didn't tell you that he was.

Vagueness is another subtle form of lying. When you confront a manipulator about something, they respond but their answer is lacking in details. They count on you not to probe them for more information.

An especially effective way to lie is to hide it in the middle of a litany of truths.

Liars lie to avoid taking responsibility or to get you to believe what they want you to believe in order to get something they want.

18. Invalidation

Invalidation is rejecting, diminishing, ignoring, judging, or making fun of someone's feelings. Invalidation is a highly detrimental form of emotional manipulation. Unfortunately, it happens all too often.

People invalidate others for a variety of reasons, sometimes purposefully and sometimes not. An abuser will use invalidation as a tool of manipulation and as a weapon. Others who invalidate may be short on empathy. Some may feel uncomfortable with your pain, or feel powerless to do anything to help you. Others may feel jealous of you for something.

Examples of invalidating statements, made in response to you expressing your feelings or talking about a difficult situation:

You should be ashamed of yourself for feeling that way.

It could be worse.

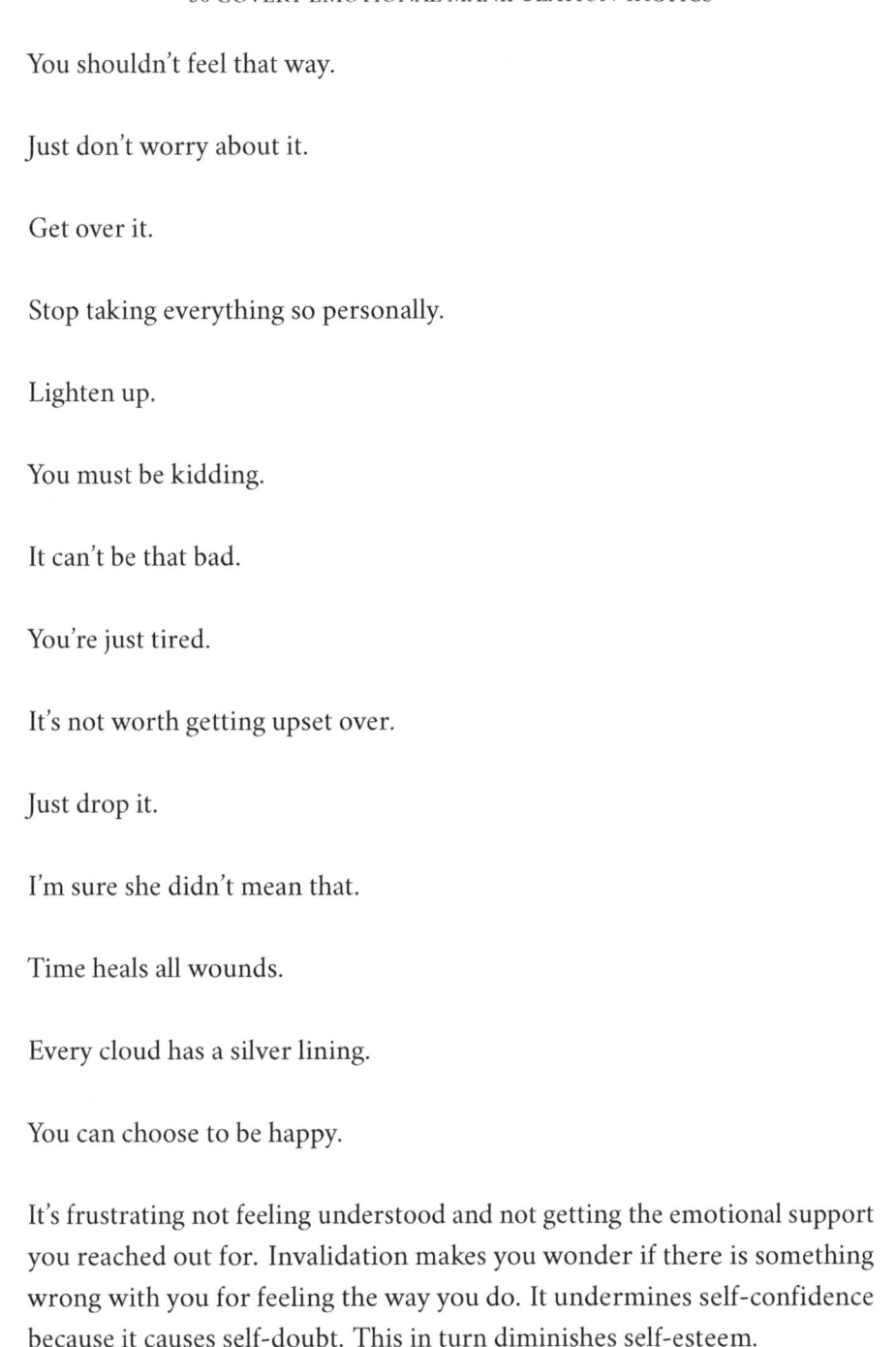

You shouldn't feel that way.

Just don't worry about it.

Get over it.

Stop taking everything so personally.

Lighten up.

You must be kidding.

It can't be that bad.

You're just tired.

It's not worth getting upset over.

Just drop it.

I'm sure she didn't mean that.

Time heals all wounds.

Every cloud has a silver lining.

You can choose to be happy.

It's frustrating not feeling understood and not getting the emotional support you reached out for. Invalidation makes you wonder if there is something wrong with you for feeling the way you do. It undermines self-confidence because it causes self-doubt. This in turn diminishes self-esteem.

Invalidation will be explored in more depth in a later chapter.

19. Charm

They know what makes us laugh, what makes us fearful, what excites us, what turns us off, and above all, what makes us vulnerable.

~ George Simon, PhD, psychologist and expert in character disturbances

Skilled manipulators excel at hiding their true character and presenting themselves as charming and seductive. If you think you would never fall for it, think again.

All of us turn on the charm and put our best foot forward in a new relationship, but manipulators use charm to advance a hidden agenda. Manipulators use charm as a way to disarm you and gain your trust. They make you feel interesting, liked, valued, and appreciated. Skilled manipulators are socially intelligent con artists adept at expressing interest in you and your welfare, and at opening up to you and appearing vulnerable.

How can you tell the difference between benign charm and malicious charm? Listen to your gut instincts, according to Dr. George Simon. On his website, manipulative-people.com, he writes "Psychopaths and the other disturbed character types... tend to exude a superficial charm or glibness in their interpersonal manner. It often goes unnoticed as the huge red flag it is... but it can be detected if you know just what to look for. The 'smoothness' or social facility these individuals display is generally not matched by congruent and concomitant emotion. They may have a very easy 'way with words'... but usually their smooth talk is not accompanied by any emotion that matches what they're saying or that can be sensed and felt by others as genuine. Still...

you can easily doubt your gut instincts (thinking that they must be being genuine) and allow yourself to be unduly swayed."

Once a malicious charmer disarms your gut instincts, you are basically defenseless.

20. Intentional Forgetting

The manipulator pretends he or she forgot something that's important to you, such as an agreement, a promise, or a commitment, or even an ingredient you need for dinner that night that he agreed to pick up on his way over. The manipulator will look you in the eye and keep a straight face as they tell you they're sorry, but they simply forgot your request or they don't recall making that agreement. When a manipulator "forgets" something that is important to you, they are attempting to evade responsibility by blaming something out of their control.

In addition, the manipulator is implying that whatever it was they forgot wasn't important enough for them to remember, and neither are you.

21. Brandishing Anger, or Traumatic One-Trial Learning

The manipulator will aim to intimidate you by putting on an act of intense, explosive anger in response to something you did or said, for the purpose of shocking you into submission. This is called traumatic one-trial learning because it instantly trains the victim to refrain from repeating the behavior that caused the outburst. What might spark such a display of rage? It is usually something that confronts, exposes, challenges, or contradicts a manipulator.

22. Scapegoating

A scapegoat is defined as a person or animal that takes on the sins of others. They are unfairly blamed for other people's problems or mistakes. A scapegoat is also known as a whipping boy or a fall guy.

Scapegoating is the process of singling out a victim and making them responsible for problems when they are not really the one who deserves the blame. A person can be made into a scapegoat for a relationship or for an entire family or even a workplace.

Skilled manipulators usually scapegoat another person on purpose, while others may unconsciously "project" their unwanted thoughts and feelings onto another to make them take the blame for their own mistakes or shortcomings, which relieves the one doing the scapegoating of shame, blame, and responsibility.

Many of the manipulation tactics in this book include an element of victim blaming, but scapegoating goes beyond that. People who are made into scapegoats feel deep and persistent shame and develop a victim mentality.

23. Belittling

A manipulator belittles a victim by using behavior or language that diminishes or mocks his or her opinions, ideas, feelings, looks, or achievements. Belittling can be accomplished non-verbally through the use of eye-rolls, scoffs, or smug smiles; and verbally by using sarcastic, condescending, or mocking tones. An abuser will sometimes disguise belittling as supposed harmless joking.

This tactic induces shame and humiliation, crushes self-esteem, and makes a victim much less willing to voice their opinions, feelings, or ideas in the future because it is not emotionally safe to do so.

Diminishing a victim's self esteem makes it easy for a manipulator to put himself in control.

24. Putting You On the Defensive

Many of the covert tactics listed here will put you on the defensive, meaning that they cause you to feel you must verbally defend who you are, what you believe or feel, or what the truth is. This is an important sign to look for when trying to determine if you are a victim of manipulation.

There is a reason manipulators want to put you on the defense. Covert manipulation tactics trigger you to react emotionally instead of responding rationally, which is exactly what the manipulator wants. Calm, rational conversations don't always go in their favor. In addition, they can then use your emotional reactions against you if they choose to, as you have seen already in several other tactics.

25. Creating Fear

What many of these manipulation tactics have in common is that they make the victim feel fear – namely, the fear of losing the manipulator and the relationship. When we don't want to lose that person, we act in the way they want us to act in order to avoid that loss.

In this situation, it is convenient that the person who created our fear is the only one who can relieve our fear, causing us to unwittingly give them all the power in the relationship. Creating fear is a powerful way to gain control. Politicians do it all the time. They create or exaggerate a potentially dangerous problem, and then tell you that if you vote for them they'll protect you from it.

26. The Pity Play

I am sure that if the devil existed, he would want us to feel very sorry for him.

~ Martha Stout, author of *The Sociopath Next Door*

Using this tactic, the manipulator will inspire your pity by making themselves look like the victim of circumstance or of some unfair person or organization. This elicits your sympathy – and your cooperation – because as a person with a conscience, you can't stand to see someone else suffering. Manipulators know how to take advantage of our conscience, compassion, and empathy.

Using the pity-play tactic, the manipulator will tell you a sad story that tugs upon your heartstrings. They might tell you they were unfairly fired from their job and need money to pay the bills, or that they've been unfairly evicted by their crazy landlord and need a place to stay, only until they find a new apartment. Oh, and the landlord kept their security deposit so they'll need to save money for another one and won't be able to help you with living expenses.

The pity play can be much more subtle. If you find out your new love interest is married but didn't say so, he or she will tell you a heartbreaking story of their spouse's emotional neglect and the terrible loneliness they have endured because of it. They will say that they only stayed in the marriage because they never imagined they would meet someone else, especially someone as wonderful as you. One crafty manipulator hung his head and said, "I gave up. I put my heart on a shelf. I never dreamed I'd fall in love again! And now here you are… I should have told you I was married, but I was so scared I'd lose you!"

Not a word of it was true, but it worked. She felt so sorry for this poor, lonely, and hopeless man who had given up on life… until she came along.

27. Rationalization

This is also known as justification or excuse-making. The manipulator creates reasons for their bad behavior that sound logical and rational, in order to make their actions appear more understandable, acceptable, or appropriate. They want to get you off their back so they can continue doing what they feel like doing.

"Every man watches porn! it's not just me."

"What I did wasn't illegal—if it were there would be a law against it, right?"

"I'm sorry I hit you. I just lost my mind for a minute because you pushed so many of my buttons."

When you trust and love someone, you strive to understand them and give them the benefit of the doubt. Manipulators are happy to help you with that.

28. Flattery

Any halfway-clever devil would decorate the highway to hell as beautifully as possible.

~ Criss Jami

You, my dear reader, are strikingly intelligent, which leaves me feeling confident that you will learn to recognize the manipulation tactic of flattery.

Flattery is excessive or false praise or compliments given in an effort to ingratiate you to a manipulator for the purpose of advancing his or her own agenda.

Manipulators use flattery because it works. We want to feel good about ourselves, so we like others who make us feel that way. When we believe someone recognizes and appreciates our good qualities, it can have a powerful effect on us.

Flattery can make you feel beautiful, intelligent, appreciated, valued, lovable, sexy, or special. You may think you would notice insincere praise and compliments, but skilled manipulators can pull it off without you noticing. If flattery accompanies an obvious ulterior motive, it's easy to spot. But if a manipulator keeps his ulterior motive hidden, it can be easy to accept as genuine. After all, if this person doesn't seem to want anything from you—if they're not selling you something, trying to get you in bed, hoping for a raise, or asking you for a loan—why would they be buttering you up?

Just as a manipulator's agenda can be kept hidden, so can their flattery. There are methods of flattery that are very subtle or craftily disguised.

One of the most subtle forms of flattery is being asked for your advice. It conveys the idea that the manipulator respects and admires your opinions, knowledge, or skill.

Another way to disguise flattery is to preface it with a disclaimer, such as "I don't want to embarrass you, but..." or "I know you won't want me to say this, but..."

Still another method of disguise is for the flatterer to disagree with your point of view at first, and then come around to agreeing with you. This technique will make you feel smart, persuasive, and heard.

Complimenting you to people you know when you're not present, with the expectation that they will pass the compliment on to you, is an effective disguise. Using this method, the flatterer avoids looking like an obvious suck-up.

When someone compliments a quality you have that is seldom noticed or appreciated by others, it's a powerful maneuver that leads you to believe the manipulator is able to recognize your best points and values them. That's just the kind of person we want in our lives. Skilled manipulators excel at reading people and figuring out their emotional needs. They also excel at pretending to fulfill them.

29. Love Bombing

Yours is the light by which my spirit's born: you are my sun, my moon, and all my stars.

~ E.E. Cummings

Love Bombing is a special form of flattery that deserves its own category. Manipulators employ love bombing to ensnare a target through a veritable *campaign* of flattery that "bombs" the target with non-stop positive reinforcement such as compliments, praise, and appreciation; declarations of once-in-a-lifetime love; spending as much time as possible with the victim; frequent phone calls, texts, and emails; gift-giving; fantastic lovemaking; and engaging in many fun and romantic activities together. It can (and does) happen strictly online as well.

What greater flattery could there possibly be than having someone who believes you're the most wonderful person they've ever known, someone who truly appreciates you and believes you are worthy of their time, attention, energy, and love? The victim is swept off their feet and straight into a relationship that will turn into the worst experience of their life.

A clue that you're being manipulated with love bombing is the rapid pace of the relationship set by the manipulator. It leaves you without time to come up for air and think clearly and carefully about who this person really is and what their motivations are. When someone declares undying love for you before they even know you, chances are good that their feelings are superficial and that they'll fall out of love with you just as quickly as they fell into it. That doesn't mean they'll move on, though; it means they may stick around long enough to devalue you slowly and methodically, for many months or even years, and cause you to devalue yourself in the process.

Your best defense is to slow the pace of any relationship that begins with such idealization and intensity. Easier said than done when you believe you've met your soul mate. Keep it in mind anyway. Remember, it takes time to get to know another person's true character. Some people are very different than who they first appear to be. We all believe we are good judges of character, but in truth we're not. There is no shortcut; it takes time and observation. Take plenty of time—at least a year, preferably more—to observe a potential partner in a variety of situations. Judge them by their actions, never by their words. Maintain your goals, boundaries, activities, interests, and relationships with family and friends. If the person really loves you (and respects you), they won't go anywhere.

Many spiritual traditions recognize that when the dark one appears he is most beautiful, most wonderful and most engaging. The truth only comes out later.

~Unknown

30. Trance and Hypnosis

Skilled manipulators can sometimes harness the power of trance and hypnosis to gain power and control. Hypnosis is simply a controlled trance. A trance is an altered mental state we enter as a common and normal occurrence, which is what makes it so easy for a skilled manipulator to induce.

When in a trance state, you are extremely relaxed and your attention is hyper-focused on a person or activity. If you've ever been so thoroughly absorbed in something that you were oblivious to distractions and to the passage of time, you have been in a trance.

We can slip into a trance from activity or stimulus with a repetitive element of movement, vision, sound, thoughts, or touch. Flickering candlelight, dance, sex, massage, video games, long drives, meditation, music, and the sound of someone's voice are all capable of inducing trance, which is highly pleasing to both the conscious and subconscious mind.

We can also go into a trance when our attention becomes narrowly focused on another person whose attention is focused narrowly on us. Psychopaths naturally focus intensely on their targets, just as a predator focuses intensely on its prey. They are very "present" when they're "interested" in someone, and that intense presence—communicated through unwavering eye contact and focused, heightened attention—can induce a similar reaction in the person who is the object of that focus. This is not done purposely; it is simply an effect of their natural way of being.

Many people say the "psychopathic stare" causes chills and a feeling of aversion. If a stranger looks at you that way in the grocery store that may be true, but if someone you're interested in or attracted to does it then it will come across as flattering interest and attention. You will likely feel captivated.

A psychopath or other skilled manipulator may also induce trance or hypnosis purposefully in order to take advantage of a victim. They may create a trancifying atmosphere with music and candlelight, speak in a slow, soothing tone of voice or engage the victim in an activity known to induce a trance state. Why would a manipulator do this? Trance and hypnosis lower our psychological defenses and leave us vulnerable to suggestion. Hypnotizing someone without their consent is considered unethical for this reason.

Increased suggestiveness makes it more likely that a victim will believe statements a manipulator makes during a trance state and that the beliefs will persist afterward. They will also have a stronger desire to repeat activities they participated in because of the heightened sense of pleasure experienced during trance. A person or activity enjoyed during trance acts as an especially persistent and powerful draw to return to the person and repeat the activity.

4

I Refuse to Have This Discussion! All About Invalidation

When we invalidate people or deny their perceptions and personal experiences, we make mental invalids of them. When one's feelings are denied a person can be made to feel crazy even when they are perfectly mentally healthy.

~ R.D. Laing, MD, psychiatrist

Invalidation is an especially damaging form of emotional abuse. Invalidation is the act of rejecting, diminishing, ignoring, judging or making fun of someone's feelings or experiences. Unfortunately, it happens all too often; there almost seems to be an epidemic of invalidation.

Invalidation is insidious and often pervasive in certain relationships. When we've had our feelings invalidated, we know that something doesn't feel right but often we can't put our finger on exactly what the problem is. One reason it remains hidden is that many of us have learned to think invalidation is normal, because it is so common. You may even do it to others. It might be common, but it's not healthy. Think of how often you've heard people say things like "it could be worse," "lighten up," "don't let it get to you," "just forget about it," or "you can choose to be happy."

People invalidate others for a variety of reasons, sometimes purposefully and sometimes not. An abuser uses invalidation as a weapon. Others may be short on empathy. Some may feel uncomfortable with your emotions or simply feel powerless to do anything to help you. Some are envious of you and will invalidate your achievements and the things that bring you happiness: "It's not such a big deal," or "He's not really that great. You could do better."

The bottom line is this: When you're invalidated, you are not having your emotional needs met because the person doing the invalidating is not behaving with empathy.

One doesn't have to operate with great malice to do great harm. The absence of empathy and understanding are sufficient.

~ Charles M. Blow

Empathy is defined as being aware of another person's thoughts and feelings, and then conveying that awareness to them in a way that creates a feeling of mutual understanding and a sense of caring. Empathy connects people emotionally.

When you tell someone close to you that you're feeling blue about something and they say, "It really isn't that bad. A lot of people have it worse, you know?" do you feel cared for, understood, and supported? Of course not, because your feelings and concerns have been invalidated. The other person has conveyed that they don't think your feelings are valid, so therefore they will not offer any support. As a result, you will not have your emotional needs met.

We all have innate emotional needs. If these needs aren't met, there can be serious consequences to our psychological health. Invalidation is no trivial matter. Steve Hein, MSW, author of the website EQI.org, calls invalidation psychological murder or soul murder.

Having emotional needs does not mean you are "needy," it means you are normal.

Our fundamental emotional needs:

To be acknowledged.
   To be accepted.
   To be listened to.
   To be understood.
   To be loved.
   To be appreciated.
   To be respected.
   To be valued.
   To feel worthy.
   To be trusted.
   To feel capable and competent.
   To feel clear (not confused).
   To be supported.
   To be emotionally safe.

You can determine the health of your current relationships by determining whether or not your emotional needs are being met.

Invalidation needs to be recognized and taken seriously because it can lead to mental health problems. Researcher Thomas R. Lynch, Ph.D., found that "a history of emotional invalidation… was significantly associated with emotion inhibition (i.e., ambivalence over emotional expression, thought suppression, and avoidant stress responses). Further, emotion inhibition significantly predicted psychological distress, including depression and anxiety."

When we experience invalidation, we defend ourselves either through withdrawal or counter-attack. "Repeated withdrawal, though, tends to decrease our self-confidence and lead to a sense of powerlessness and depression. On the other hand, going on the offensive often escalates the conflict. A healthier response, one which is both informative and assertive, without being aggressive, is to simply express your feelings clearly and concisely. For example, you might respond, 'I feel invalidated,' 'I feel mocked,' or 'I feel judged,'" says Hein. How someone responds to those statements is important. Do they invalidate you again when you say you feel invalidated, or do they want to learn more?

The following are examples of invalidating statements.

Statements such as these either minimize your feelings, deny your perceptions, order you to feel differently, tell you how you should feel, or put you on a guilt trip for thinking or feeling the way you do:

I thought we already talked about that.
   I can't believe you're going to bring that up again.
   I refuse to have this discussion.
   You should be ashamed of yourself for feeling that way.
   You need to realize how lucky you are.
   It could be worse.
   You shouldn't feel that way.
   Think about those who have it worse.
   Just don't worry about it.
   Get over it.
   Stop taking everything so personally.
   Get a life.

Lighten up.
Cheer up.
Don't look so serious.
You've got it all wrong.
Of course I respect you.
But I do listen to you.
That is ridiculous.
This is nonsense.
That's not the way things are.
I honestly don't judge you as much as you think I do.
You are the only one who feels that way.
It doesn't bother anyone else, why should it bother you?
You must be kidding.
It can't be that bad.
You're just tired.
It's nothing to get upset over.
It's not worth getting that upset over.
You should feel thankful that _____.
You should be glad that _____.
Just drop it.
You should just forget about it.
I'm sure she didn't mean that.
Maybe he was just having a bad day.
You shouldn't let it bother you.
I'm sure she means well.
Don't make that face!
You don't really mean that.
Do you think the world was created to serve you?
Don't you ever think of anyone but yourself?
What about my feelings?
Time heals all wounds.
Every cloud has a silver lining.
Life is full of ups and downs.

You can choose to be happy.
You are just going through a phase.
Everything has its reasons.
Everything is just the way it is supposed to be.
This is really getting old.
This is getting to be pathetic.
I am sick and tired of hearing it.
You should be over that by now.
It's not such a big deal.
That's what you're so excited about? Is that all?
You think too much.
Don't let it get to you.
That's nothing to be afraid of.
Stop feeling so sorry for yourself.
You've been upset about this for too long; it's time to move on.
Just don't think about it.
You need to get past that.
You need to get on with your life.
You're _____ (jealous, insecure, crazy, unstable, a worry wart, overly dramatic, a complainer, too sensitive)
You're making a big deal out of nothing.
You're imagining things.

Invalidation can also be conveyed without words. Non-verbal invalidation includes such actions as giving the silent treatment, shrugging the shoulders, or rolling the eyes.

With increased awareness, you'll begin to notice invalidating comments and behaviors.

Invalidation makes us wonder if there is something wrong with us for feeling the way we do. According to Hein, "It seems fair to say that with enough invalidation, one person can figuratively, if not literally, drive another person crazy… This is especially possible when one person has long-term power or influence over another."

How someone responds to your emotions, experiences, and perceptions will indicate how much they respect you, how much they care about you and your feelings, how capable they are of empathy and intimacy, and if they are trying to change you or control you.

> *Having emotional needs does not mean you are "needy." It means you are normal.*

5

The Most Powerful Motivator on the Planet

There is nothing like the bliss and elation of new love, especially when you believe you've found "the one." That takes it to another level. You may feel you never truly knew what love was before meeting this person whom you believe is your soul mate. You experience incredible joy and happiness. Your feel as if this love was written in the stars, that it was meant to be, and meant to last forever.

But one day something unexpected happens. You get a queasy feeling that you cannot shake. You sense deep in your gut that the man or woman you love is pulling away, but you do not know why. Your heart sinks and your stomach clenches with fear.

In the process of a pathological relationship, the moment when the joy at finding love turns into the fear of losing it is called the manipulative shift. When that happens, the manipulator takes control. The person who idealized you now devalues you. A long and painful downhill ride begins.

Fear takes away our ability to think clearly. It's an intensely powerful and uncomfortable emotion, and we want to feel safe again. In this case, fear is caused by the threat of losing who we believe is our loving and wonderful partner.

When we feel fear, we will give just about anything to the person who can take that fear away. In this situation, that person is the very one who caused it in the first place—the manipulator. He or she can take our fear away by becoming attentive and loving again, and we try hard to regain that attention and love. The manipulator shows us how—and keeps us hooked on them—through the use of covert manipulation.

If fear is something we want to avoid, how does a manipulator use it to keep us hooked?

By alternating fear with another extremely powerful emotion: Love.

Creating fear of losing the relationship—and then relieving it periodically with episodes of love and attention—employs a powerful tactic of manipulation known as intermittent reinforcement.

Those positive episodes that banish our fear release a potent dose of feel-good hormones and neurotransmitters including dopamine, which induces euphoria.

Have you ever gone to a casino and played a slot machine? You feed in quarters and pull the handle, over and over, and watch colorful images of fruit and numbers and bells whiz by. If you don't win anything you start to fear that you might lose all the money you already put in, let alone not win the jackpot, so you are compelled to keep trying. What if you walk away from this machine now and the next person to sit down pulls the handle and wins? You insert a few more quarters, pull the handle and—amazingly—three identical images of red cherries align, bells ring, and colorful lights flash. Quarters pour out from the machine and into your waiting hands. This reward causes your brain to light up, too, by releasing a burst of pleasure-inducing dopamine, and you want more. Your fear vanishes; you have your money back. And now that you have all those shiny quarters there's no reason not to keep playing! Who knows, maybe you'll win the jackpot! You start feeding the machine again. You alternate between the thrill and relief of winning small jackpots and the fear of losing it all. You're hooked.

Psychology researchers have long considered intermittent reinforcement the most powerful motivator on the planet. It is also the most maliciously manipulative tactic. Intermittent reinforcement is simply unpredictable random rewards in response to repeated behavior, but there is no more powerful formula to get someone to feel or act in a desired way. It can be elevated gradually to extreme levels, creating compliance that is obsessive and even self-destructive. You won't notice it for what it is when it's happening… unless you're aware of the tactic and how it works.

In a manipulative relationship, the more infrequently the crumbs of love are offered, the more hooked you get. You become conditioned, like a rat in a laboratory cage. When rats are taught to press a lever that randomly dispenses a delicious morsel, they press the lever obsessively. After a while, they will keep pressing the lever even if no more morsels come out… until they starve to death (I think this is an unconscionable experiment, by the way). Similarly, we may hold on to a partner and a relationship when there is no more love to be had.

Lab rats are taught to press the lever by starting them out with continuous positive reinforcement. Think of it as "treat bombing" in place of "love bombing." When the experiment begins, every time the rat presses the lever she gets a morsel. Then the researchers change the game. The rat presses the lever but a morsel isn't delivered with every press anymore, only on random presses. The rat is fearful that she won't get fed but she knows pressing the lever brought food in the past, so she keeps pressing it until she gets some. As long as she gets a morsel every once in a while, she keeps pressing it. When the morsels stop coming, she's sure she'll get one next time she presses it, or the time after that... so she never stops trying.

It works the same way in a manipulative relationship. You are the rat, and the morsel you keep trying for is love.

Intermittent reinforcement plays a big role in the phenomenon of traumatic bonding. A trauma bond is a very strong attachment to an abuser that develops not in spite of manipulation and abuse, but because of it.

Powerful emotional attachments are seen to develop from two specific features of abusive relationships: power imbalances and intermittent good-bad treatment, according to psychology researchers Donald G. Dutton and S. Painter, "Emotional attachments in abusive relationships: A test of traumatic bonding theory," *Violence and Victims,* Volume 8, 1993.

Intermittent reinforcement begins insidiously. The stage of continual positive reinforcement—love bombing—ends. Perhaps a phone call or text message isn't returned or doesn't come at the usual time. A hand that always held ours as we walked down the street is kept in a pocket instead. We witness our partner flirting with someone else, although they deny it. For a week, they aren't in the mood to make love. They subtly or overtly criticize or demean us for our weight, our age, our ideas or opinions, or some quirk they once claimed to love. They compare us unfavorably to someone else. They give us the silent treatment.

Little by little, it gets worse. Much worse. But there are always the times you are given a few morsels of love: your partner reverts back to being the loving and attentive person they used to be. All hope is not lost! You're unwittingly put on an emotional roller coaster, riding it to dizzying heights that alternate with death-defying drops.

What can you do to prevent being victimized by intermittent reinforcement? It's hard to recognize if you know nothing about it, but now you're armed with knowledge. Here are some things to keep in mind for future relationships:

Consider the trustworthiness of your partner on an ongoing basis. Once he or she gains your trust, it's very easy for them to get away with a lot of bad behavior. After all, you have a solid image of them as trustworthy. But trust shouldn't be given once and then last forever. A person's trustworthiness should be re-evaluated as needed. How can you tell if your partner is still deserving of your trust?

Trust is based on three aspects: Predictability, dependability and faith. Predictability is the consistency of your partner's behavior, and predictable behavior is in stark contrast to the unpredictability of intermittent good-bad or hot-cold treatment. Dependability is the degree to which you trust your partner to be honest and reliable. Faith represents your conviction that your partner will be responsive to your needs and can be counted on to behave in a kind and caring manner.

Don't judge your partner's trustworthiness by how they were in the past—consider the three elements of trust at the present time. Skilled manipulators are good at gaining our trust, but not so good at keeping it. They count on our image of them as trustworthy as a substitute for actually being trustworthy.

Keep in mind the signs in yourself that you're being manipulated, which you learned previously in chapter two, 'How to Tell if You're Being Manipulated." You will not feel like that in a healthy, normal relationship. Those signs are reliable indicators that intermittent reinforcement and other manipulative tactics are at play.

Look for the hallmarks of a healthy relationship: emotional intimacy, commitment, consistency, balance, progression, shared values, love, care, trust, and respect.

Listen to any alarm bells that go off in your head, and listen to friends and family members who you know to have your best interests at heart. Don't ignore them, no matter how much you would like to.

Become and stay conscious of the power balance of the relationship. The person who cares less has the power. Be aware that when you feel chronically insecure, heartsick, anxious or hurt, you can get caught up in the drama of abuse and become blind to the larger dynamic at work. Is this a healthy relationship, one that you're thriving within, or not?

Ask yourself if your relationship is based on real emotional intimacy or if you're being tricked into accepting intensity as a substitute. Find out how to answer that question by reading the next chapter.

Powerful emotional attachments are seen to develop from two specific features of abusive relationships: power imbalances and intermittent good-bad treatment.

~Psychology researchers Donald G. Dutton and S. Painter

6

Intimacy or Intensity? A Relationship Litmus Test

I have flown and fallen, and I have swum deep and drowned, but there should be more to love than 'I survived it.'

~ Lisa Mantchev, So Silver Bright

It seems that magic has entered your life. It brings you once-in-a-lifetime, soul-mate love, true romance, and amazing sex. You are swept off your feet and taken to an enchanted world just for two, one that floats like a bubble high above the mundane world below.

You never expect this bubble to burst. You believe the incredible intensity you share with your partner indicates a deep connection, one that will last a lifetime. Falling in love is a heady experience that has the potential to become a strong and lasting connection based on emotional intimacy.

That can't happen if your partner isn't incapable of emotional intimacy, though.

You may not even notice a lack of true intimacy if you're dazed and deluded by the extraordinary intensity of your experience. The smoke and mirrors of manipulation can easily distract you from the truth.

Intimacy is based on trust, understanding and vulnerability. People who become emotionally intimate do so by taking the risk of being emotionally vulnerable with their partner, revealing their true selves and feeling emotionally safe afterward instead of feeling judged, mocked, invalidated or rejected.

Intimacy is based on emotional safety, patience, respect, consistency, and a mutual give-and-take. Without self-disclosure, there can be no intimacy. The more intimate you are with someone, the safer you feel and the more worthwhile the relationship. You are free to be yourself within an atmosphere of mutual acceptance and understanding.

Intensity, on the other hand, involves drama, anxiety, uncertainty, and fear. It's all about push-pull, hot-cold, high-low.

According to Harriet Lerner, PhD in her book, *Dance of Intimacy*, "Intensity is being completely lost in the emotion of unreasoning desire. It is marked by urgency, sexual desire, anxiety, high-risk choices and the reckless abandonment of what was once valued. All-consuming euphoria similar to recreational drug use (addictive chemical reactions in the brain).... loss of ability to make rational evaluations of what is true, valuable and worthy. Desire to be always close to that person at any cost."

In contrast, Lerner writes that an intimate relationship "is one in which neither party silences, sacrifices, or betrays the self and each party expresses strength and vulnerability, weakness and competence in a balanced way... Intimacy means that we can be who we are in a relationship, and allow the other person to do the same. 'Being who we are' requires that we can talk openly about things that are important to us, that we take a clear position on where we stand on important emotional issues, and that we clarify the limits of what is acceptable and tolerable to us in a relationship."

That is simply not possible with a manipulator.

Bonding created by intensity—emotional highs and lows—is maintained by powerful surges of euphoria-inducing dopamine during the highs, and an intense craving for more during the lows.

Learning theorists have found that a pattern of intermittent reinforcement, which is positive reinforcement alternated with punishment (a pattern of abuse and reward), develops the strongest emotional bonds.

Intermittent good-bad treatment triggers biological changes as well as emotional ones. Relationships based on intensity are actually the same as an addiction to drugs or alcohol. Interaction with your partner fosters a specific pattern of compulsive behavior and is not really an intimate relationship at all: It's an addiction, in the true sense of the word.

These exploitative relationships form a trauma bond, a highly addictive attachment to a person who is hurting you. A person in a trauma bond is essentially addicted to a relationship with someone who is destructive and hurtful. Signs of a trauma bond include the inability to detach and self-destructive denial.

Writer and abuse survivor Amanda Domuracki described it perfectly when she wrote, "We cannot walk away, though, because without us realizing it, our abuser has become our human needle; our Drug Lord of Love. The person who owns our self-value and self-worth and who, in the name of love, can reject us into deep lows with a single glare, or send us to euphoric highs with one simple smile."

To know that you are loved for who you are, and to know someone else in all of their vulnerability and to love them as they are, may be one of life's most fulfilling experiences, says sociologist Brene Brown.

Intensity, on the other hand, is the opposite of fulfilling. It is draining, exhausting, crazymaking and, ultimately, meaningless and empty.

The most important test of intimacy is to ask yourself if your relationship is a safe haven where you feel loved and accepted for being yourself.

7

Your Basic Rights In Relationships

You possess inherent basic rights within your personal relationships. Manipulators work hard to make you forget what they are, so remember to ask yourself periodically if you are exercising your rights in your close relationships, and if your rights are being respected. Doing so can help you identify whether a relationship is a healthy one or not. It can also help you spot a good relationship gone bad, much sooner than you might have otherwise.

I have the right to have my needs and feelings be as important as anyone else's.

I have the right to experience and express my feelings, if I choose to do so.

I have the right to express my opinions, if I choose to do so.

I have the right to set my own priorities.

I have the right to establish independence if I choose to.

I have the right to decide how I spend my time.

I have the right to choose my own lifestyle.

I have the right to change my lifestyle, myself, my behaviors, my values, my life situation, and my mind.

I have the right to make honest mistakes and to admit those mistakes without feeling humiliated.

I have the right to self-fulfillment through my own talents and interests.

I have the right to grow as a person and to accept new challenges.

I have the right to choose who I spend my time with and who I share my body with.

I have the right to be treated with dignity and respect in all my relationships.

I have the right to be listened to respectfully.

I have the right to ask for what I want assertively.

I have the right to say "I don't understand" or "I don't know" without being humiliated.

I have the right to say "No," and to set limits and boundaries without feeling guilty.

I have the right to set limits on how I will be treated in relationships.

I have the right to expect my boundaries to be respected.

I have the right to walk away from toxic or abusive relationships.

YOUR BASIC RIGHTS IN RELATIONSHIPS

I have the right to have these basic rights in my relationships and to stand up for them.

Empowering, isn't it? Your basic rights in relationships are also the foundation of your personal boundaries. If you keep these rights in mind and defend them, you will not easily become a victim of emotional manipulation.

8

Now What?

I would find the path out of the labyrinth.

~ Carlos Ruiz Zafón, *The Angel's Game*

Realizing that manipulation is behind the pain and confusion you've experienced in a relationship can be a shocking discovery. Becoming aware of it is only the first step. You may find yourself going back and forth between certainty and doubt, which can come at you from multiple directions: yourself, your confidants, and from the manipulator, who will seldom admit the truth. You might find that you repeatedly analyze every detail of what happened yet are unable to settle on one point of view. It is no small matter to suspect that your partner, spouse, or someone else close to you could be a remorseless manipulator, so it is no surprise if you wonder if your assessment is accurate. Even if you believe it is accurate, it is a difficult truth to accept. Victimization by a manipulator can be a major life trauma.

There are no easy answers as to what to do next. The way you respond depends on many factors: Is the person who is manipulating you a pathological manipulator who has no other way of relating to others? Or is it someone who uses manipulation from time to time to get some need met, who could learn a better way to go about that? What is your relationship to the manipulator? How detrimental are the effects of their manipulation? What have the consequences been to the relationship, and to your psychological, emotional, spritual, and physical well-being?

If you're involved with a pathological manipulator, the only answer may be to end your relationship with them. That might not be easy to do. You might be married to the manipulator and have children together. But there may be no other answer if you are truly dealing with a destructive manipulator who might have a personality disorder such as psychopathy or narcissistic personality disorder, which at this time are believed to be impossible to treat. It is wise to reach out to a mental health professional who understands emotional manipulation and abuse, along with the trauma it can inflict, for guidance and support. Contacting your local domestic violence organization can be helpfull as well. Emotional manipulation is abuse.

The following books can help you to learn more about pathological manipulators.

Dangerous Personalities: An FBI Profiler Shows You How to Identify and Protect Yourself from Harmful People by Joe Navarro and Toni Sciarra Poynter.

From the book description: "Former FBI profiler Joe Navarro shows readers how to identify the four most common 'dangerous personalities' and analyze how much of a threat each one can be: the Narcissist, the Predator, the Paranoid, and the Unstable Personality. Along the way, readers learn how to protect themselves both immediately and long-term—as well as how to recover from the trauma of being close to such a destructive force."

In Sheep's Clothing: Understanding and Dealing With Manipulative People, by George K. Simon, PhD:

Dr. Simon is an excellent source of information about the character-disordered among us and how to deal with them.

From the book's description, included are "Four reasons why victims have a hard time leaving abusive relationships; power tactics manipulators use to push their own agendas and justify their behavior; ways to redefine the rules of engagement between you and an abuser; how to spot potential weaknesses in your character that can set you up for manipulation; and 12 tools for personal empowerment to help you maintain greater strength in all relationships."

Who's Pulling Your Strings? How to Break the Cycle of Manipulation and Regain Control of Your Life, by Harriet Braiker, PhD:

This is a book everyone should read. The author teaches readers how to handle many different types of manipulation. Her tactics are not meant to be used on pathological manipulators, but they can help you to understand, deal with, and change the behavior of the more garden-variety, less destructive manipulators in your life.

"Indispensable advice for anyone who wants to protect themselves from manipulation: Work on developing clear, strong personal boundaries. Boundaries protect your values, goals, time, resources, emotional health and whatever else is important to you. Manipulation causes you to act against your own best interest. If your boundaries are clear and strong, you will recognize when someone is attempting to cross them. The goal of manipulation is to rob you of what is of importance and value to you, for the manipulator's personal gain. Please don't let that happen to you."

For guidance in developing your personal boundaries, I've written the book *Boundaries: Loving Again After a Pathological Relationship.* Many readers have found it to be a helpful and valuable resource.

Made in the USA
Coppell, TX
13 October 2021